If you've ever pondered the true identity of Puss in Boots, been frustrated trying to contact your bank, wondered why grey geese fly south or wanted to know what Santa thinks about Christmas, here is where you'll find the answers.

Pelicans Can't Read is a collection of comic verse and limericks on these and other diverse subjects, such as the vagaries of the English language or how to tell dragons apart.

Also by Patricia Feinberg Stoner

At Home in the Pays d'Oc

Tales from the Pays d'Oc

Murder in the Pays d'Oc

Verse

Paw Prints in the Butter

PELICANS CAN'T READ

Patricia Feinberg Stoner

with illustrations by

Bob Stokes

and

Bob Bond

Fascom

Published in the UK by Fascom 2022
Copyright Patricia Stoner 2022

The rights of Patricia Feinberg Stoner to be identified as author of this work have been asserted by her in accordance with the Copyright Designs and Patents Act 1988,
All rights reserved.

ISBN 978-1-7397379-0-0

Cover image by Bob Stokes
www.bobstokes.co.uk

Additional illustrations by Bob Bond
www.footballershappen.com

Cover design by Natasha Murray
https://nmurray3004.wixsite.com/mysite-1

For Himself and the Girls

CAVE CANEM

A response to John Keats' ode

'On first Looking into Chapman's Homer'

I little know of Stout Cortez
or whether, as the poet says,
you can descry the blue Pacific
From Darien. To be specific
I only know one thing, to whit:
you'll surely get your ankles bit
should you unwisely vantage seek
by trying to stand upon a Peke.

GREY GEESE

Hush, my baby, don't you cry
It's only grey geese flying by.

We are the grey geese, gladsome tribe,
Flying south with happy faces
Child-free to exotic places.
Flying south with joyful cries
To dalliance under foreign skies.
We are the grey geese, gladsome tribe.

We are the grey geese, merry band.
Tyranny of school terms past
We've sold the caravan at last.
No longer good old Mum and Dad
We travel fancy-free and glad.
We are the grey geese, merry band.

We are the grey geese, joyful we:
No more a slave to childish voices
We make our selfish, grown-up choices.
The wide world beckons: Paris, Rome
We have no need to hurry home.
We are the grey geese, joyful we.

We are the grey geese, free of chains.
Now the childcare days are done
We frolic in September sun -
Now at last we've got the chance -
In Turkey, Tuscany and France.
We are the grey geese, free of chains.

We are the grey geese, happy breed
Working days at last behind us
Sitting in the sun you'll find us
Coloured postcards gaily sending
To kids whose rightful due we're spending.
We are the grey geese, happy breed.

Hush, my baby, don't you cry
It's only grey geese flying by.

FORBIDDEN LOVE

Of all my loves I love you more
Than any I have loved before.

Your salt is sweeter far than honey
Your worth cannot be prized in money.

When I unwrap your golden form
A strange desire in me is born.

When I but taste your fragrant flesh
My senses are at once refreshed.

Although I know our love is wrong
I'm helpless: its's for you I long.

Although I know it's wrong to yearn
I can't resist, for you I burn.

Though you pile pounds on waist and hips
Oh, how I love you, fish and chips!

THIRD AGERS, TAKE A BOW!

From gentle walks to Spanish
Third Agers take a bow.
Even if you're gran-ish
We're all Third Agers now.

We're learning, fast and furious,
All subjects great and small.
The clever and the curious
Find groups for one and all.

If you've a taste for country dance
Or hear the siren call
Of Poetry, come join us
For we're Third Agers all.

The comma called Oxford's the pits.
I rank it with herpes and zits.
   I'm sure not amused
   When I see it used:
Quite frankly, it gets on my nerves.

      Cried an angry young lady from Goring:
      'My boyfriend's incredibly boring.
         Uninspiring in bed,
         And, what's more,' she said
      'I can't get to sleep for his snoring.'

On the new *Autouroute des Plages*
If you meet a girly, curvy and large,
   Who says '*Veux-tu, chéri?*'
   Don't go thinking it's free:
The transaction is strictly *péage*.

      Cried an out-of-work actress: 'Disaster!
      I've broken my leg, it's in plaster.'
         Said her agent: 'Too bad.
         Still, she ought to be glad
      That someone has finally 'cast' her.

An elderly lady from Norwich
Ate a five-kilo packet of porwich.
   Was it greed? Not at all:
   Her flat was so small
She simply did not have the storwich.

      Propositioned, a trendy Madame
      Said '*Non*!' to a randy *gendarme*.
         'It just isn't chic
         Having sex with a *flic*,'
      She explained with a trace of alarm.

Michael Flanders encountered a gnu.
Not, as you'd expect, in a zoo.
   Rustington by the sea
   Where he happened to be
Can seemingly boast of one too.

      My Purdey, a dog with no bounds,
      Is quite the most avid of hounds
         For anything offered,
         And if it's not proffered
      She'll steal it, and claim it was found.

TRIOLET 1: TO MY DOG

Don't think you've got the upper paw
Because your eyes are wide and brown
And puppy-soft, and cute, and more,
Don't think you've got the upper paw.
Don't think that you can break the law
And creep beneath the eiderdown.
Don't think you've got the upper paw
Because your eyes are wide and brown.

TRIOLET 2: MY AUNT MEG

I went to visit my Aunt Meg
She's rich as Croesus, and as tight.
I went to visit, not to beg.
I went to visit my Aunt Meg
I'd rather die than stoop to beg
But as my bank account is slight
I went to visit my Aunt Meg
She's rich as Croesus, and as tight.

A POEM FOR OUR TIME

I tried to phone my bank today,
I needed some advice:
My account was nearly overdrawn
Which wasn't very nice.

A charming young man answered me:
'Good morning, I'm Sanjay.
I'm at your service, ma'am,' he said,
'How may I help today?'

I told him what the problem was.
'Just let me check,' he said.
I waited for a quarter hour
And then the phone went dead.

I tried to get my bank online
But when I pressed the key
'This website can't be shown' is what
The damn thing said to me.

I tried to go and see my bank,
I had to take a train,
But when I got there, it was closed
So I'd struck out – again!

And now I'm badly overdrawn
I know just who to thank.
For that, my friends, is what you get
When you try to phone the bank.

PELICANS CAN'T READ

I was strolling in Saint James' Park, and minding my affairs,
And I hadn't got no worries, and I hadn't got no cares.
The sun was shining hot, like, on my head, so I decided
To sit down by the lakeside on a bench that was provided.

It wasn't long before I felt the urge to feed my face
So I unwrapped a small pork pie I'd brought along in case.
Well, I heard a sort of scuffle, but I didn't pay no mind,
And no-one thought to tell me what was creeping up behind.

First thing that I knowed about it, there was this long beak
Come poking over me shoulder and it give me pie a tweak.
Gave me quite a start, it did: I looked up in amaze.
There stood a great big pelican before my startled gaze.

'Gerroff!' I shouted, 'Gercha!' But the pelican declined.
It was staying where the grub was, it had quite made up its mind.
We'd gathered quite a crowd by now and someone shouted 'Shame!
The poor thing must be starving, else it wouldn't be so tame.'

I knew, of course, that this was bosh: they get fed reg'lar, like,
By a little man with bags of fish what comes by on his bike.
Besides, there's signs about such things, I've noticed quite a few
That tell the people in the park the things they mustn't do.

Like: 'Please don't feed the pelicans, it don't do 'em no good.
In fact, there's some has snuffed it cos of eating dodgy food.'
Now I'm rather tender-hearted, though you might think me absurd,
And the last thing that I wanted on me conscience was this bird.

So once again I yelled at it: 'Why don't you bugger off
And catch a fish, you feathered twit? This ain't your kind of scoff.
Push off!' I cried, 'You'll come to harm, and I'll be held to blame.'
The pelican ignored my words and scoffed it just the same.

So what's the use of notices, and signs that say 'Don't feed'?
You can tell the people all you want – but pelicans can't read.

MUSINGS ON A RAINY DAY

(with apologies to Ogden Nash)

If there's one thing in this world I hate more than any other thing it's umbrellas.

Not on ladies, of course, because ladies as we all know have to keep their hair dry, but when it's fellas

well, then, I think they look poofy.

And they may be as handsome as Micky Mouse or as ugly as Goofy

but to me they're a nuisance and, worse than that, they're a menace,

because if I want to get past a chap with an umbrella I have to walk in the gutter or else flatten myself against the fenace.

And if I don't do either of these things, then my eye will get poked.

Which is why I feel choked.

And I tell you the last thing in this world that's calculated to give me the jollies

is fellers with brollies.

So let's all get together and rid the world of this peril

and if a chap should get stroppy about it, why then we'll kick him in the ferrule.

ERMINTRUDE: A CAUTIONARY TALE

Ermintrude was very sweet:
She didn't pout or stamp her feet
Or throw her dollies from the pram
Or smear the walls with strawb'ry jam.

But truth to tell she had one flaw
Which got her parents on the raw:
If they set out for anywhere
She'd mutter: 'Are we nearly there?'

It made her mother tear her hair
And filled her father with despair
When Ermintrude, with anxious air
Would ask them: 'Are we nearly there?'

No matter if they'd set their hearts
On pleasant jaunts to distant parts
The journey they must needs curtail
When Ermintrude began to wail.

They tried all sorts of cute devices:
They offered sweets, they offered ices.
They gave her pretty picture books
But all were met with darkest looks.

It made her mother tear her hair
And filled her father with despair
When Ermintrude, with anxious air
Persisted: 'Are we nearly there?'

It chanced one day in early spring
They set off for a seaside fling.
They'd planned, with quite a lot of glee,
A week at Brighton by the sea.

But they had hardly gone a mile
When Ermintrude – she's such a trial! –
Began in her accustomed way
To ask about their ETA.

It made her mother tear her hair
And filled her father with despair
When Ermintrude, with anxious air
Persisted: 'Are we nearly there?'

Her father then got so distracted
He hit the steering wheel and cracked it!
The car veered left, the car veered right
And crashed, it was an awful sight.

The three lay tangled in a heap
They were quite dead, they weren't asleep.
Harsh retribution, I declare
For simply asking 'Are we there?'

So hearken, children, everywhere
When on a journey have a care.
Don't fill your father with despair
Don't make your mother tear her hair
By asking 'Are we nearly there?'

There was an old maid of Verdun.
As haughty a miss as they come.
   She was so supercilious
   You'd think she was bilious
Or had something stuck up her bum.

      There's a bar in the town of Auxerre
      That's run by Barthélémy *frères*.
         They'll ply you with whisky
         Until you feel frisky
      Then sell you their sister, *pas chère*.

While driving along the A40
In a little red car that was sporty,
   Jim remarked to Suzette:
   'How about it, my pet?
Let's find a lay-by and get naughty.'

      A myopic young fellow named Ron
      Once picked up a girl in Narbonne.
         'She' was really a lad,
         But his sight was so bad
      He never detected the con.

While walking one day in the *Bois*
Michelle and Jean-Pierre went too far.
  Now she nurses the *bébé*
  Saying ruefully, 'Mébé
I should have retained my *sang froid.*'

      A pious young lady from Trinity
      Was taking a degree in divinity.
        But she went on the town
        With a fellow named Brown
      And unfortunately lost her lecture notes.

A novice who leapt on a horse
Was soon filled with gloom and remorse.
  'What possessed me,' he cried,
  To think I could ride?'
At which the steed threw him, of course.

      A cheerful young fellow named Trev
      Once went for a romp in Lodève.
        But he soon lost his smile
        When he caught something vile
      In a house of delight called *Mon Rêve.*

IMPATIENCE

When I was young, I said to Mum
When will the blessed future come?
(I wasn't allowed to say bloody).

When I was young, I said to Dad
When it does I'll be flipping glad
(I wasn't allowed to say f*****g).

Now I'm old and getting grey
The flipping future's here to stay
(I don't like to say f*****g).

Now I'm old and getting stout
The future I could do without
(And I know it will be bloody).

So children, hold your horses, do:
The future's on its way for you.
And when you get there you will mourn

The good old days that now you scorn.
You may rant and swear and cuss
You'll still get older, just like us.

TUSK A SONG AT TWILIGHT…

Come, let us sing the praises of the warthog.
Though rarer than your common bacon-and-pork hog
The wart-hog's praises are too rarely sung.

The creature, let's admit it, is no beauty -
No poet would describe him as a cutie –
And yet he's sensitive and highly strung.

A cruel joke of nature made him ugly
When deep inside his heart is warm and snuggly
As witness his devotion to his young.

For though you might consider it a giggle, it
's so sweet to see the love he shows the piggle-let.
The hardest heart could not remain unwrung.

So greet the wart-hog warmly as a fellow!
So treat the wart-hog kindly as friend!
For underneath the warts, the hide, the tusks,
The warthog's really human, just like us.

January 16th is Dragon Appreciation Day

DRAGON CASTE

The Imperial dragon, the prince of the blood
To which our traditions are owed,
Can be seen at a glance to be lord of them all:
Imperial dragon -- five toed.

And how do you ascertain a dragon's rank?
Count the claws, dear, count the claws.
How tell the monarch from the mountebank?
(I've said it before) count the claws.

The Mandarin dragon is second in line.
Though not as elite as the first,
Four claws on his paws his degree clearly show:
By no means of dragons the worst.

And how do you ascertain a dragon's status?
Count the claws, dear, count the claws.
How to tell which one is second-rate is
(I've said it before) count the claws.

The thrice-digital dragon -- that's three-toed to you --
Who was wont upon maidens to dine,
Got a lot of PR from his fight with St George
But he's last in hierarchical line.

And how do you ascertain a dragon's caste?
Count the claws, dear, count the claws.
How tell which should be first and which the last?
(I've said it before) count the claws.

Five, four and three, the dragon's claws
Assign to each his place.
But dragons, whether great or small
Are still a noble race.

Does it matter what a dragon's caste is?
Damn the claws, dear, damn the claws.
Of snobberies, I think the nastiest
Is counting claws, dear, is counting claws.

THE TYRANNY OF CATS

The sun of southern France beat down
And forced us to retreat.
In the kitchen, sipping wine
We sheltered from the heat.

Then suddenly my husband said
'Look! There's a cat in here.'
And I replied, as wives reply,
Indulgently: 'Yes, dear.'

Had he, I wondered, drunk too deep?
The wine was strong, I knew.
Or had he simply nodded off
And dreamed? But it was true:

To catch the slightest breath of air
The kitchen door stood wide;
The cat had seen a welcome there
And slipped unseen inside.

It stood and mewed, as cats will mew,
And with imperious stance
It clearly said, 'Now give me milk.'
And thus began the dance.

For such a merry dance he led
Us, all that summer through.
He'd but to voice a whim and we
Obeyed, as humans do.

At crack of dawn he would appear
And yowl until we rose.
We gave him milk, we gave him fish
And cuddles – when *he* chose.

But summer passed as summers will
And it came time to leave.
'What will become of him?' I sobbed.
There was no need to grieve.

When he saw suitcases come out
(He knew what they were for)
Without a backwards glance he left
And found a bed next door.

For cats are independent folk.
They don't need us, and that's
The deep, mysterious secret of
The tyranny of cats.

SPARE A THOUGHT FOR SANTA

'God rest ye merry gentlemen!' I hear the people say.
They're getting all excited cos it's nearly Christmas day.

It's time I got a move on, and never mind me feet,
Me chilblains, me lumbago, nor rain, nor snow, nor sleet.

OH - I'm harnessing me reindeer and loading up me sleigh,
And putting on me muffler, cos Santa's on his way.
Ho ho ho.

Hey, Rudolph! Where's 'e gone, then? I bet I flipping knows:
He's skived off down the boozer with 'is boozer's flipping nose.
(Why d'you suppose it's rose? It's pink from drink!)
Ho ho ho.

OH - I hates the flipping chimneys they never thinks to sweep
And all the pussyfooting while the kiddies is asleep.

And I hates the flipping driving, especially after dark,
And it isn't always easy to find a place to park.

And while we're on the subject, I think it's pretty thick
All this flying round the country when air travel makes me sick.

BUT I'm harnessing me reindeer and loading up me sleigh
And pulling furry boots on cos Santa's on his way.
Ho ho ho

Oh, it's time I joined a union -- A Santa's TUC --
But it wouldn't really work, cos there's only one of me.

And that's another matter that gets me on the raw:
Them flipping understudies you see in every store.

It's not as if I minds it when I sees me face to face
In Morrison's or Tesco's -- or any flipping place --

But where's the recognition for a job I've done so long?
And, come the New Year honours, why don't I get a gong?

STILL, I'm harnessing me reindeer and loading up me sleigh,
And filling a hot bottle cos Santa's on his way.
Ho ho ho.

There's just one ray of comfort that stops me feeling sore:
Me working year's a day long, and the hol's three sixty-four!

So spare a thought for Santa as you feast and play and dance.
I'll be celebrating Christmas in the sunny south of France.

OH - I've unharnessed all me reindeer and emptied
out me sleigh.
Come wine! Come song! Come women!
Cos Santa's on his way.

Ho ho ho
    H-hiccup
        (scuse me).

A LADY TAKES ISSUE WITH HER LOOKING GLASS

Mirror, mirror on the wall
That doesn't look like me at all.

That raddled hag in you I see
I'm pretty sure it isn't me.

My cheek is smooth, my eye is bright
Yet in your depths I look a fright.

The lines you show I have not got:
My skin is flawless, not a blot.

But wait! I feel a nagging doubt:
That vision I could do without,

Could it be true? Could I be she
Whom in the mirror's face I see?

OK, mirror on the wall
Perhaps it is me after all.

A PUSS IN BOOTS

In the high-street chemist yesterday
Upon a thoughtfully-provided chair
Beside a radiator sat
A large and well-contented cat.
The chance was far too good to miss
For one who loves a play on words
So: 'Look! A Puss in Boots! I cried.

The shopping zombies clearly thought me mad.
They turned, as only English people turn,
A blank and even hostile stare
Upon me, standing foolish there
As 'Look! A Puss in Boots!' I cried.

But then the creature stretched and purred
And opened amber eyes (that matched its fur).
And then it turned and winked at me.
I'll swear I saw it wink at me.
As 'Look! A Puss in Boots!' I cried.

BISCUIT MUSINGS

I could burble through a bourbon with a cheerfulness of mien.

I could gobble up a ginger nut and I love a gypsy cream.

A pink and crumbly wafer is the very thing for me

And jammy dodgers on a plate bring nothing short of glee.

I like an amaretto when I'm feeling European

Nice biscuits, though, aren't really nice, in fact they're rather mean.

That also goes for Rich Tea bics: they're dry and they are frightful

But chocolate fingers make my day and hobnobs are delightful.

I like biscuits when I'm tranquil, I like biscuits when I'm restive,

And if I'm feeling miserable there's nowt like a digestive.

I'm talking through a biscuit so forgive me if I mumble.

I've filled my mouth with cookies and that's the way they crumble.

AS SHE IS SPOKE

Envy the student of German or French,
Those languages writ as they're spoke,
But mourn for the fellow who labours in vain
The spelling and speech to drive into his brain
That are mastered by anglophone folk.

Some examples are here and I'm sure you'll find more
Of how English is sadly perverse.
Two words you'll encounter that look just the same
But spoken so differently no one can blame
The student who utters a curse.

If something moves your daughter to delighted girlish laughter
Or you hear the wind wind softly through the boughs;

If a rough cough is distracting while the players take a bow
And a fiddler to the plaudits waves his bow;

If you love to move beside the cove and spy a pear tree near,
Or wander like a gander through the grass;

Or if alone you like to stroll and none knows where you've gone
And you meet a lord who wants to have a word;

And you know that he's a poser but if you look a little closer
He's nothing but a loser you can tell.

If you wonder what lies yonder and you stop to have a ponder
Or you want to scale the heights by half past eight;

If you hover like a lover with a feeling that it's over
Or call yourself a shaker and a mover;

You're neither a student of German nor French
It's English you learn, sad to tell.
The grammar is quite simple, it's the spelling that confuses
And pronunciation seems to go the way it damn well chooses.
And so ends my ditty –farewell!

FROM THE PEN OF RICHARD PATTERSON

Richard Patterson is a fictional English poet who lives in the south of France,

and in the pages of 'The Jabberwock Continuum' by Patrick J Stoner

and in 'Tales from the Pays d'Oc' and 'Murder in the Pays d'Oc' by Patricia Feinberg Stoner.

He has a verse for every occasion.

THE DINER, THE THIEF
AND THE INDIAN PRAWN

There was a diner and he loved his food
Sing hey nonny, nonny, nonny no.
There was a thief who was up to no good
Singing hey nonny, hey nonny no.

Said the diner one day to his wife dear and true:
'I fancy an Indian supper, do you?
I've a tandoori craving for chicken and spice
So if you'd call the take-away, that would be nice.'

So his wife, all obedient, called the Monsoon
And said to them 'Please bring our dinner quite soon.
Mixed grill for my husband, a dansak for me,
With rice and parathas and some onion bhajis.'

And soon the meal came, with aromas delish.
There was chicken and keema kebab on his dish
And -- the thing that the diner loved most in his life
(Second only of course to his dog and his wife) –

To his beaming delight in the tandoori there sat a
Succulent prawn in the midst of the platter.
Said the diner 'I'm saving this morsel for last:
It's just what I like to conclude the repast.'

But did he but know it, a thief was about:
A four-footed felon with burglarious snout.
She lovingly snuffed up the smell of the food:
For tandoori grill she was just in the mood.

Her master ate quickly, 'twas almost too late,
And she didn't once take her brown eyes off his plate.

Then a scheme popped up into the ne'er do well's head:
With a shriek she leapt up, to the back door she fled.

She barked and she barked. Such a noise did she make
That the man left his dinner – a foolish mistake.
He hurried to open the garden door wide
So the vigilant dog could patrol the outside.

But cunning, oh cunning! The dog rushed about
And back through his legs she returned. With a shout
Of terror and anguish the man saw his prawn --
But just for an instant, and then it had gorn!

For tripping on tiptoes the felon did snare
The prawn from the plate that the diner left there
And fled to the kitchen, a smile in her eyes.
Where she munched and she munched on her ill-gotten prize.

A moral there is to this tale I relate:
Never leave unattended the meal on your plate.
No matter how loudly you hear the dog bawl
Keep your eye on your prawn or you'll lose it – that's all.

So if you're a diner and you like your food
Sing hey nonny nonny nonny no
Beware of the thief who is up to no good
Singing hey nonny hey nonny no.

A-SITTING ON A BENCH
(dedicated, with apologies to Lewis Caroll, to the Good Ol' Boys of every French village)

I'll tell thee everything I can
Concerning matters French,
And of an aged, aged man
A-sitting on a bench.

'Who are you, aged man?' I cried,
'And tell me why you sit
Upon a bench in Morbignan.
Pray, what's the sense in it?'

He said 'I'm old, as you can see
My days of toil are done.
And so I'm here upon my bench
A-sitting in the sun.'

Just then another four came up
And stood beside the first.
And cried 'The café beckons us
For we've an awful thirst.

'And if you care to stand us, sir,
A *rouge*, or a *demi*
We'll gladly tell to you our tale.
For ancient men are we,

And we have laboured in the fields
And tended of the vine
And so to rest upon our bench
We think it right and fine.'

I took those ancient, ancient men
Across the road to drink.
But, sadly, when they'd drunk their fill
In torpor they did sink.

And so I never heard the tale
Explaining why the French
In dotage like to pass their time
A-sitting on a bench.

If you enjoyed Pelicans…
you might like Paw Prints

PAW PRINTS IN THE BUTTER
Patricia Feinberg Stoner

"If you have a cat, know a cat or have ever interacted with a cat, this collection of poems will have you chuckling'

- *Ingénue Magazine*

Printed in Great Britain
by Amazon